# THE CLEVER TODDLER
## COLORING BOOK

Copyright © 2020 Kenzth Art

ISBN: 9798645358457

# This Book
## Belongs To

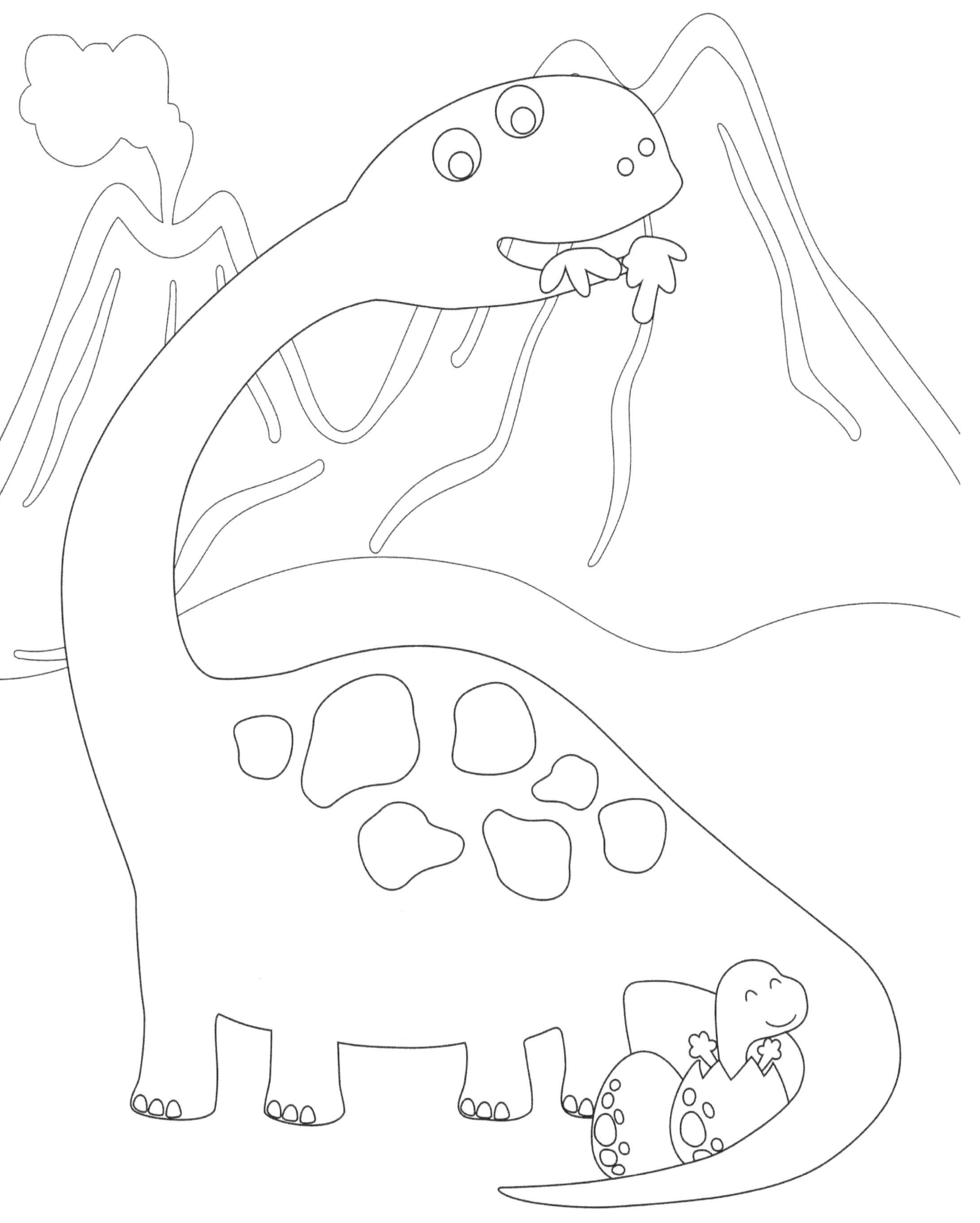

Papa!!

ToW
TRUCKS
5

S
is for
sailor

TO THE
RESCUE

P
is for
penguin

funny animals
CIRCUS

I love Music
Yeah..!
75

# D is for dino

Wood
land

funny
SURFER

B
is for BEAR

canoe
club

is for
Monkey

S
is for
sheriff

my
best
friends

canoe
festival

tiger
go to
school

MOTO
7
7
SPEED
250cc

ROUND
2

BASKETBALL
Players

CROCO
3
1

whats
up dab?
DANCE
ALL
DAY

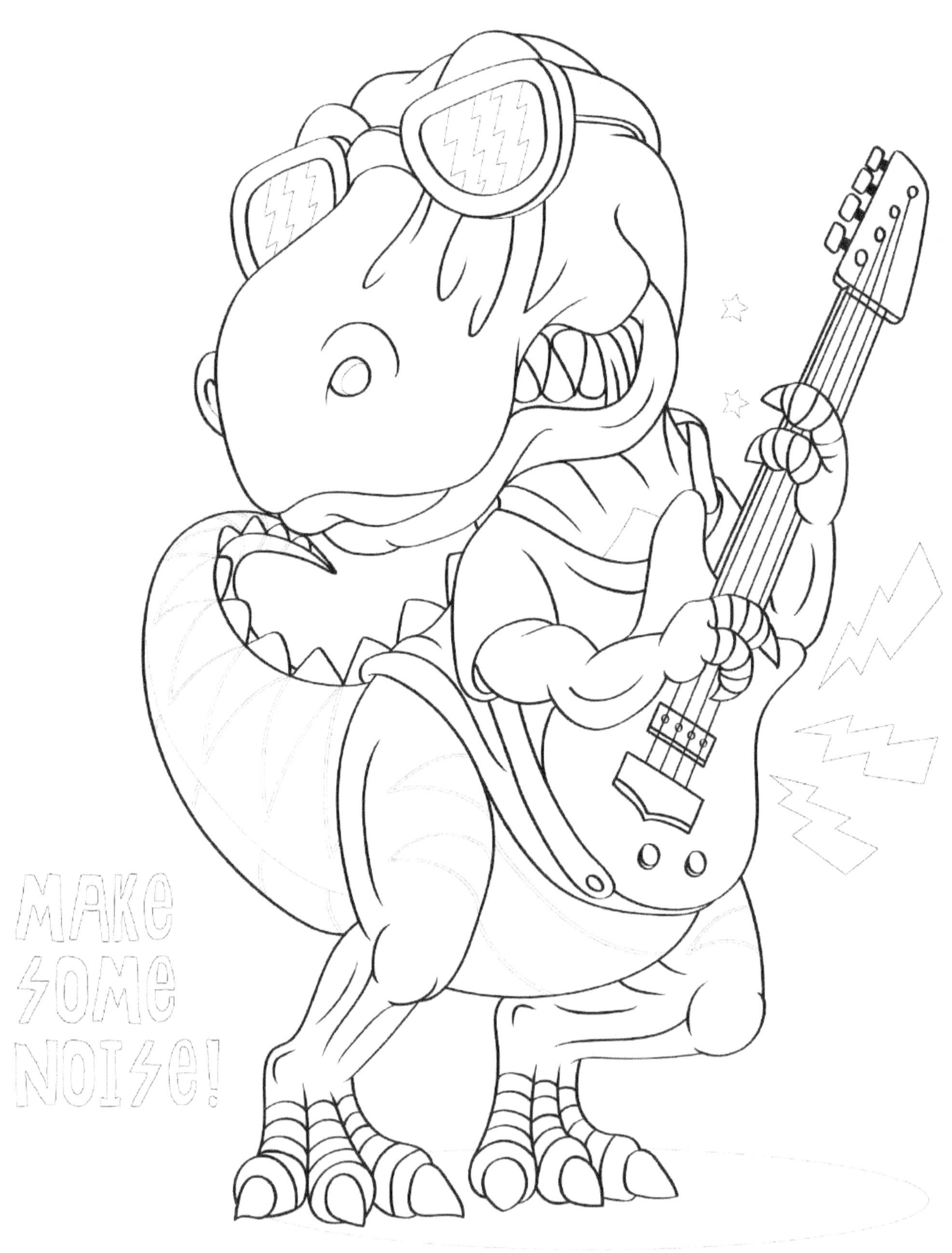

MAKE
SOME
NOISE!

YEAH!
YEAH!

SURF
YEAH!
LIFE GUARD

SURF
YEAH!

SUPER COOL!
NYC

YEAH!
CROC

YEAH!
MAKE SOME NOISE!
POLICE LINE DO
CROSS